AF506952

DECODING THE SYSTEM:

What Every Parent Should Know About Public Schools and Neurodiversity

JANEL WOODARD

Decoding the System: What Every Parent Should Know About Public Schools and Neurodiversit.

Copyright © 2026 by Janel Woodard

All rights reserved. No part of this book may be reproduced or transmitted in any form or by any means without written permission from the author.

ISBN: 979-8-9987951-3-8

Printed in the USA by A'Lure Publishing, LLC

(alurepublishing.net)

For my son—

You have always seen the world a little differently, and that has been one of your greatest strengths—even on the days it didn't feel that way. This book exists because of you. I wrote this so you would grow up knowing your mind is powerful, your voice matters, and your differences are not something to overcome—but something to protect.

May you always understand your rights, recognize your worth, and never doubt that you belong in every room you choose to enter.

Know that I am always in your corner, cheering you on, believing in you, and proud of the person you are becoming.

With all my love,

Mom

PREFACE

I never imagined I'd have to fight so hard just for my child to be understood. What began as a few "concerns" from teachers evolved into a years-long battle for the support my son rightfully deserved. Interactions with school administration became increasingly frustrating: conversations became meetings, meetings became evaluations, and soon I was in a world that spoke a language I didn't recognize. Acronyms, scores, reports—each providing a piece to the puzzle but not the entire vibrant picture of my son.

I'd sit on conference calls, my coffee gone cold, listening to people describe my child as if he were a problem to be solved. They focused on behavior; I concentrate on capability. The way he taught himself basketball dribbling tricks at the age of 2. The spark in his eyes when he understood something in his own way. The gap between what they measured and what I knew widened with each passing day.

If you're reading this, you probably know that feeling. The frustration of watching your child struggle in a system not designed with them in mind. The nights replaying every conversation, wondering if you pushed too hard or not enough. The exhaustion that seeps into your bones when every small victory feels like it came at the cost of your sanity.

I wrote this book because I've been there. I've sat in the tiny plastic chair across from administrators, my hands shaking as I tried to explain for the fifth time that my child isn't defiant, isn't broken, isn't less. He's different. And different deserves to be understood, not fixed.

Over time, I learned the rhythm of the system—the paperwork maze, the coded language, the faces that soften when you stop fighting and start connecting. Most importantly, I learned how to document without losing heart, how to advocate without burning out, and how to trust my instincts more than the forms that tried to define my child.

This book is the guide I wish I'd had at the beginning.

It isn't a step-by-step manual. It's a real-world guide — drawn from trial, error, and persistence.

Inside, you'll find tools, templates, and plain-language explanations for the parts that can feel impossible to decode. You'll learn how to recognize when your child needs support, how to prepare for meetings, and how to make sure what's promised on paper turns into real change in the classroom.

But more than anything, I hope this book gives you what I once needed most: proof that you're not alone. There's strength in the questions you ask, wisdom in the way you see your child, and power in refusing to give up.

Every child deserves more than to simply get by—they deserve to be seen, celebrated, and understood for who they truly are.

Welcome to Decoding the System. Let's begin.

Janel Woodard

Content

PREFACE   **4**

Content   **8**

CHAPTER 1   **10**

WHEN SOMETHING FEELS OFF   10

CHAPTER 2   **15**

DISCIPLINE OR DISCRIMINATION?   15

CHAPTER 3   **24**

WHY NEURODIVERSITY—AND WHY IT MATTERS   24

CHAPTER 4   **37**

THE CLUES WE MISS   37

CHAPTER 5   **47**

GETTING ANSWERS   47

CHAPTER 6   **66**

KNOW YOUR RIGHTS USE YOUR VOICE   66

CHAPTER 7   **81**

THE FOUR STEP SYSTEM THAT CHANGED
EVERYTHING   81

CHAPTER 8   **94**

BUILDING A SCHOOL TEAM THAT WORKS   94

CHAPTER 9   **102**

ADVOCACY IN ACTION   102

CHAPTER 10   **112**

RAISING A SELF-ADVOCATE   112

CHAPTER 11   **123**

LIVING THE PLAN AT HOME AND SCHOOL   123

CHAPTER 12   **133**

GRACE FOR THE JOURNEY   133

CONCLUSION   **146**

YOU ARE THE CONSTANT   146

REFERENCE   **156**

APPENDIX A   **160**

RESOURCES AND TEMPLATES FOR
PARENTS   160

CHAPTER 1

WHEN SOMETHING FEELS OFF

I had a typical pregnancy—until the 41st week, when my son arrived just one day before his scheduled induction. Looking back, I should've known then he'd do things on his own terms.

From day one, I was all in—the kind of mom who barely let her baby out of sight. He was calm, joyful, and easygoing. He reached each milestone with ease, and I cherished them all. But by age two, something shifted. While his motor skills were strong, his speech lagged. At first, evaluations reassured me there was nothing to worry about. Still, I knew something wasn't quite aligning.

By age three, his personality changed. Tantrums became a daily routine. I chalked it up to sibling anxiety as I prepared to welcome our second son. Then the daycare notes started. I told myself he was just a late bloomer—or that I was overthinking. But deep down, I knew better.

At four, we enrolled him early in kindergarten. I knew it was a stretch, but childcare costs left us no choice. The signs showed up quickly: daily disruptions, difficulty focusing, repeated calls from the principal's office. Eventually, we pulled him out and tried again the following year. The behavior didn't stop. And when I asked for help, the school told me to wait it out. "He's young." "Boys are just like that." But I could see his frustration growing. He was trying—and failing—not because he wasn't capable, but from lack of support.

That's when guilt crept in. I blamed myself. Maybe too much play time. Perhaps I missed something important. Maybe it was the divorce, or the move, or the chaos of change. But finally, the pediatrician said the words: ADHD.

When I got the diagnosis, I felt a wave of relief... followed immediately by overwhelm. Now what? We did everything: therapy, tutoring, structured routines. But school still felt like a daily battle. Teachers said, "He's smart, but..." while I struggled to translate "potential" into progress. I didn't even know what to ask for—let alone how to demand it.

I learned about MTSS, then 504 plans, and eventually wrote a formal request myself. But even with a plan in place, support was inconsistent. Then the pandemic hit. Overnight, I became both mom and teacher. And it was then I truly saw how my son learned—what helped, what didn't, what exhausted him, and what lit him up. By the time he returned to in-person learning, it was clear: even with a 504 plan, it still wasn't enough.

If you're reading this, maybe you've felt the same: confused, exhausted, unsure where to turn— but still fighting for your child. I wrote this book for you. To share the roadmap, I had to build from scratch. To decode the acronyms, translate the red tape, and remind you that you're not crazy, you're not alone—and you're not asking for too much.

You're asking for what your child deserves.

CHAPTER 2

DISCIPLINE OR DISCRIMINATION?

Before diving into the heart of this book, we must first confront the elephant in the room. The hard truth is that discrimination still lives in our school systems. It doesn't always look like the obvious kind—sometimes it hides behind low expectations, unequal discipline, or subtle decisions about who gets support and who doesn't. For parents like us, especially when raising neurodiverse children of color, those quiet inequities can have a lasting impact.

I remember the first time I sensed it with my son. I couldn't prove anything, but deep down I knew that if he were a different color or if his needs looked a little more familiar to the teachers, we might not be fighting this hard for understanding. It was a feeling that sat heavy in my chest—a mix of anger, sadness, and hopelessness. That realization changed how I approached advocacy forever.

Children with disabilities and children of color are often disciplined more harshly than their peers for similar behaviors. Reports from the U.S. Department of Education and the U.S.

Commission on Civil Rights show that although students with disabilities make up only about one in six public school students, they represent nearly a third of all suspensions. They're also twice as likely to get referrals to law enforcement as their non-disabled peers. For many students, those missed classroom hours send a message that they don't belong—and that message lingers.

The same pattern shows up when it comes to access. Students who are neurodiverse or from marginalized backgrounds are often under-identified for evaluations and overrepresented in disciplinary statistics. Research from Columbia Teachers College (2021) found that while students with disabilities make up roughly 13% of the student body, they represent only about 4% of dual-enrollment and 2% of Advanced Placement enrollments nationwide. In plain terms, that means the system isn't giving equal access to opportunities that can shape futures.

Even when students do qualify for supports through a 504 Plan or IEP, implementation often falls short. Missing accommodations, untrained teachers, or disciplinary consequences for disability-related behavior can all violate federal law. The Individuals with Disabilities Education Act (IDEA) requires schools to review student behavior and link it to the disability before disciplinary removal. Similarly, Section 504 of the Rehabilitation Act prohibits punishing students for behaviors that stem from unmet accommodation needs. Too often, these protections exist on paper but not in practice.

For families of color raising neurodiverse children, bias operates on multiple levels. Research shows that Black and Latino students with disabilities are both under-identified for services and overdisciplined once identified. I've seen this firsthand in how people describe behavior, the tone they use in meetings, and the assumptions they make before fully understanding the situation. This difference is where discrimination becomes more than policy failure—it becomes personal.

These numbers aren't just statistics to me. They show up in the stories I hear from other moms all the time. My Black mom friends often ask, 'Where do I even start?' because they're still fighting to have their concerns taken seriously. My White mom friends, even those new to advocacy, often share how the school reached out first, offering testing or support before they had to ask. Some might say it's just about being in the right district, but after years of moving and changing schools, I've learned: bias doesn't stop at the district line.

No school—regardless of its ranking— is fully insulated from the broader social and structural forces around it. The difference is whether they choose to confront it or let it persist.

Educators know how to spot academic challenges, but they don't always consider the whole picture. Large class sizes, inconsistent training, and unconscious bias all influence how educators interpret behavior. For example, teachers may label a Black or brown child as 'defiant' while describing the same behavior from another student as 'energetic' or 'creative.' The data shows this clearly: Black students are more likely to face disciplinary actions for subjective behaviors like "disrespect" or "disruption," even when the underlying issue is academic frustration or unmet needs (U.S. DOE, 2022).

That's why your perspective as a parent is essential. You see patterns that teachers can't. You witness the nightly homework battles, the tears, the exhaustion. Those observations are valid evidence when you start the process of requesting evaluation or support.

Turning Awareness Into Action

Discrimination in education isn't only unjust—it robs children of their most basic right: the right to learn in an environment that values who they are. As parents, we can't always change the system overnight, but we can hold it accountable step by step. That starts with understanding your rights, documenting what happens, and speaking up consistently.

Here's what I learned along the way:

- Keep detailed records—emails, meeting notes, report cards, and discipline logs. Patterns tell a story that schools can't ignore.

- Don't hesitate to ask for written clarification when something feels off. If a decision doesn't align with your child's plan, request an explanation in writing.

- Build alliances with teachers and staff who "get it." Allies inside the system often become the most significant catalysts for change.

- And when you feel tired or unheard, remember that advocacy is both personal and collective. Every step you take for your child opens the door a little wider for another.

Bias exists within the system—but so does the power to change it. That change starts with awareness, persistence, and the courage to keep showing up.

CHAPTER 3

WHY NEURODIVERSITY—AND WHY IT MATTERS

For most of my life, I witnessed schools operate around one definition of "normal." Sit still. Follow the rules. Learn this way, at this pace. Anything else meant something was wrong. But once I began advocating for my son, I discovered that the real story is far more complex—and far more beautiful.

Neurodiversity simply means that human brains are naturally different. We all think, learn, and process information in our own ways. That's not a flaw—it's a reflection of the diversity built into humanity itself. Some of us think in pictures, others in patterns, rhythms, or stories. Some focus intensely, others make connections quickly across ideas. When we honor those differences instead of trying to "fix" them, we create a more inclusive and effective learning environment for everyone.

The term neurodiversity was first introduced in the late 1990s by sociologist Judy Singer and has since reshaped how educators and parents view conditions such as ADHD, autism, dyslexia, and others. Rather than labeling these as disorders, the neurodiversity movement reframes them as variations within the human experience—a reminder that there is no single "right" way to think or learn (Baumer & Frueh, 2021; Singer, 1998).

In classrooms, neurodiversity means some students may need quiet spaces to read while others learn best when they can move or talk through ideas. One child may struggle to write but can build or code complex systems from memory. These differences remind us that brilliance doesn't always look like straight-A report cards—it shows up in creativity, problem-solving, and persistence.

Rethinking "Normal" in the Classroom

The traditional school model emphasizes long periods of sitting still, minimal movement, and uniform instruction. But modern research challenges that idea. Studies show that prolonged sitting can reduce focus, energy, and comprehension (Pontifex et al., 2021; Mainsbridge et al., 2019). In contrast, even short activity breaks—stretching, standing, walking—can boost attention, mood, and memory (Webster et al., 2015; Edutopia, 2022).

We've known for years that adults need breaks from meetings and screens; the same is true for kids. I saw this firsthand during remote learning. When my son could stand, fidget, or walk around while working, his focus improved dramatically. Yet schools still expect many children to sit for nearly eight hours a day. It's no wonder attention struggles exist everyday—it's a model designed for uniformity, not humanity.

Even in the workplace, studies from Cornell Health (2021) show that movement and regular pauses improve performance and reduce stress. If adults need that flexibility, how can we deny it to children who are still learning to regulate their bodies and emotions?

Common Types of Neurodiversity

Every neurodivergent profile is unique, but here are some of the more recognized types educators may refer to when developing supports or accommodations:

ADHD (Attention-Deficit/Hyperactivity Disorder): Involves differences in attention, focus, and impulse control. Many children with ADHD are creative, quick-thinking, and curious—but thrive best when routines include structure and movement.

Autism Spectrum Disorder (ASD): Characterized by differences in social communication, sensory processing, and behavior.

Autism exists on a broad spectrum—some children need intensive support, while others are highly independent but still face unseen challenges.

Dyslexia: A language-based difference that affects reading, spelling, and sometimes writing. Many dyslexic learners have exceptional strengths in spatial reasoning and visual creativity.

Dyscalculia: Involves difficulty with number sense and mathematical reasoning.

Dysgraphia: Affects handwriting, organization, and written expression.

Sensory Processing Differences: Influence how a child experiences sounds, sights, textures, or movement—sometimes causing discomfort or overwhelm in loud or bright environments.

Executive Functioning Differences: Affect organization, time management, emotional regulation, and planning. These are critical life skills, but often go untaught in schools.

When my son was first identified with ADHD, I initially believed the label defined him. Now, I understand it only described how his brain works, not who he is. Once we accepted that, we could finally focus on his strengths: his creativity, humor, and ability to think differently.

In education, a learning disability (LD) refers to challenges in one or more basic psychological processes involved in understanding or using spoken or written language. These challenges may appear in reading, writing, speaking, or math. Under the Individuals with Disabilities Education Act (IDEA), students with specific learning disabilities are entitled to specialized instruction and supports through an Individualized Education Program (IEP).

IDEA lists 13 categories of disabilities that can qualify a child for special education services, including Specific Learning Disability (SLD), Autism Spectrum Disorder, Speech or Language Impairment, Emotional Disturbance, Other Health Impairment (OHI, often including ADHD), and others. Each state applies these categories using its own procedures—some rely on discrepancies between ability and performance, while others use a response-to-intervention (RTI) model. You can find your state's definitions and policies on its Department of Education website under Special Education Services.

Understanding these terms doesn't mean memorizing legal jargon. It means learning the system's language so you can speak it with confidence. When you know what "accommodation," "evaluation," or "eligibility" actually mean, you're no longer a bystander—you're a partner in the process.

Breaking Myths and Defining Key Terms

Misconceptions about learning differences persist, and they can be especially damaging for children who already feel misunderstood. Let's dismantle a few of the most common ones:

Myth: "A learning disability means my child isn't smart."

Truth: Intelligence and learning style are not the same. Many neurodiverse students have average or above-average intelligence. Their challenge lies in how they process information, not their ability to understand it.

Myth: "ADHD is just bad behavior or lack of discipline."

Truth: ADHD is neurological, not moral. Punishment rarely works because the struggle isn't about willpower—it's about regulation. Support, structure, and empathy make a bigger difference than discipline.

Myth: "They'll grow out of it."

Truth: Neurodiversity is lifelong. Children don't outgrow their wiring, but they can learn to manage challenges and build on their strengths.

Myth: "Accommodations give an unfair advantage."

Truth: Accommodations don't lower expectations—they remove barriers.

They ensure equal access so that every child has the opportunity to succeed.

Once I began seeing my son's brain as different—not broken—everything changed.

Understanding neurodiversity gave me language to describe what I was witnessing and the courage to push back when systems didn't. It helped me see that his differences didn't limit his strengths—they shaped them.

When you understand how your child learns, you stop trying to fit them into the system and start helping the system fit them.

Action Steps for Parents

1. Reframe the narrative at home.

Use strengths-based language with your child: "Your brain works differently, and that's not a bad thing. It means you need different tools, not less potential."

2. Learn your child's neurotype.

If your child has a diagnosis (or you suspect one), take time to research how their brain processes the world. Start with trusted sources like Understood.org, ADDitudeMag.com, or local advocacy centers.

3. Create a "Learning Snapshot."

Write down what you observe about how your child learns best. Think: What helps them focus? What triggers frustration? This insight can become a valuable advocacy tool for meetings with teachers and schools.

4. Introduce the concept of neurodiversity to your child.

Keep it age-appropriate, but don't hide it. Let your child know their brain is unique—and valuable.

5. Challenge "normal."

The next time you hear or think, "Why can't they just sit still/pay attention/stay organized?"—pause and ask: "Does this expectation align with how their brain is wired?

CHAPTER 4

THE CLUES WE MISS

At first, I was utterly opposed to having my son tested for anything. I honestly believed it was just another attempt to label a young Black boy and push medication as the solution. I stood firm in that belief for years. Eventually, though, I decided to explore medication further — a decision that took time, reflection, and experience. That's a conversation that I always say, do what works best for your child and your family.

Looking back, the first real step was accepting that acknowledging my child's challenges didn't mean he was "less than" or imperfect. As parents, it's natural to want to believe our children are fine — that they'll "grow out of it" or that others just don't understand them. I had to let go of that mindset. I learned that recognizing my child's needs didn't diminish him; it empowered both of us. Even with his challenges, he is still my child — deeply loved and perfectly himself.

In those early daycare years, I was the mom saying, "Not my baby." But over time, I began to see the patterns — the same behaviors happening at home were also showing up in the classroom. That's when I had to confront the truth.

So, let me hold your hand and tell you this: if you find yourself resisting the idea that your child might need support because of your own fears or ego, you might unintentionally be standing in their way. Denial doesn't protect them — it delays their progress.

This chapter isn't about labels. It's about awareness. It's about listening closely to your child's experience and recognizing patterns that might signal a need for additional support. Early identification can change everything—it can mean the difference between years of frustration, like us, and the start of meaningful progress.

Every parent knows their child best. We know their smiles, their rhythms, their little quirks that make them who they are. So when something feels off—when school becomes a struggle instead of a place of growth—we often sense it before anyone else does. The problem is that schools too often tell us to 'wait and see.' To be patient. To give it time. But waiting rarely makes things better when a child is falling behind or feeling unseen.

For me, the signs were clear once I knew what to look for. Recognizing these patterns was the beginning of understanding — not just for my son, but for me as a parent learning how to advocate for his success. My son showed the telltale signs of Attention-Deficit/Hyperactivity Disorder (ADHD), including:

- Inattention: Difficulty focusing or completing tasks.

- Hyperactivity: Constant movement or restlessness, always "on the go."

- Impulsivity: Acting without thinking, blurting out answers, or interrupting others.

- Forgetfulness: Frequently misplacing items or missing essential details.

Often, the first signs of a learning difference or neurodiverse need are subtle. Teachers might describe your child as "bright but inconsistent," "easily distracted," or "not living up to potential." Homework might take hours longer than it should. Mornings before school may turn into meltdowns, stomachaches, or tears.

Sometimes, these signs appear not as academic struggles, but as behavioral or emotional ones. A child who feels misunderstood might withdraw, act out, or start saying things like "I don't want to go to school" or "school is too hard." These are not signs of laziness or defiance — they're signals of frustration and unmet needs.

While every child's experience is different, these are signs I wish I had recognized earlier. You don't need to see all of them — even a few consistent challenges are worth exploring.

Academic Signs:

• Persistent trouble with reading, writing, or math despite extra help.

• Forgetting what they've learned from one day to the next.

• Strong verbal skills but difficulty with written work.

• Avoidance of homework, reading aloud, or school discussions.

Behavioral and Emotional Signs:

• Frequent meltdowns around schoolwork or transitions.

- Complaints of headaches or stomachaches before school.

- Sudden drop in confidence or motivation.

- Teachers describing your child as "unfocused," "lazy," or "unmotivated."

Social and Communication Signs:

- Struggles to make or keep friends.

- Difficulty reading tone, facial expressions, or social cues.

- Frustration when misunderstood or rushed to respond.

Physical or Sensory Clues:

- Sensitivity to light, noise, clothing textures, or crowded spaces.

- Constant movement or fidgeting seems to help concentration.

- Challenges with coordination or handwriting.

When you start noticing these patterns, it doesn't mean something is "wrong" with your child—it means something in their learning environment isn't matching how they process the world.

For many children, academic frustration turns inward. They begin to think, I'm just not smart enough. They start to withdraw, shut down, or act out. I remember the breaking point came not during a test, but one evening at the kitchen table. He looked up at me from his homework, tears welling, and said, "Mom, I'm trying. I just can't do it." That moment shattered me—but it also woke me up. He didn't need more discipline; he needed understanding and support.

When your child starts showing distress around learning, don't ignore it. Emotional reactions are communication. Frustration, anxiety, or avoidance often reveal deeper struggles—like unrecognized dyslexia, ADHD, or sensory challenges. Trust what you see.

When to Request a Closer Look

If you've seen consistent struggles in one or more of these areas, it may be time to request an evaluation through the school or a private provider. Here's a simple checklist to help guide that decision:

☐ My child continues to struggle in reading, writing, or math despite extra support.

☐ Homework or studying leads to frustration, tears, or avoidance.

☐ My child's teacher notes inattention, disorganization, or inconsistent performance.

☐ My child's behavior at home differs significantly from reports at school.

☐ My child shows anxiety or emotional distress related to schoolwork.

If you check several of these boxes, don't wait. You can write a formal letter to request an evaluation under the Individuals with Disabilities Education Act (IDEA) or Section 504 of the Rehabilitation Act. Early action matters—the sooner we identify a need, the sooner we can put appropriate supports in place.

CHAPTER 5

GETTING ANSWERS

By sixth grade, we made a tough call: he would live full-time with their father. We hoped a new environment would help reset things. Instead, his challenges escalated—more distractions, more behavioral issues, and over ten suspensions. It was one of the hardest years we had faced.

Then came the breaking point: an in-school suspension for a minor infraction he wasn't even directly involved in. And that's when the real lesson began.

Without informing us, the school scheduled a Manifestation Determination Meeting (MDM) to determine whether my son's behavior was directly related to his disability. If not, the school could push for a change in placement, including alternative or even disciplinary schooling.

When we found out, our answer was immediate: Absolutely not.

We pushed back. I called out the lack of intervention. At the same time, his father escalated to the superintendent. We chose action over passivity and became relentless. That meeting wasn't just about our son. It was about stopping a pattern that too often pulls neurodiverse kids, especially Black boys, into a pipeline that labels instead of supports.

I share this because knowing our rights and speaking up kept him from being pushed further into a system that punishes difference rather than understanding it. During that process, one of the school psychologists—an incredible advocate—suggested something we hadn't considered: autism. That moment reframed everything. Years of confusion started to make sense.

It was a turning point. And if you're navigating something similar, this may be yours, too.

So, I jumped into action, calling specialists, chasing evaluations, and doing the research all over again. It wasn't easy—waitlists stretched for months, sometimes a year. But I refused to stop until we had answers.

Finally, in the summer of 2024, I got the call. We took our son to the Carolina Institute for Developmental Disabilities at UNC for an evaluation. And on a warm summer day in July, after hours of testing and interviews, we finally received the clarity we had been fighting for:

- Semantic Pragmatic Communication Disorder

- Autism Spectrum Disorder (ASD)

- ADHD, Combined Type

- Anxiety

It explained everything—from social confusion to emotional overload to the brilliance that didn't always show up on paper.

And just like that, everything changed. I had spent years advocating on instinct. But once I had documentation—once I had evidence—I had leverage.

The lesson? **Don't wait to start the evaluation process.** If your gut says something's off, listen. You don't need permission to advocate. You need clarity— and the sooner you seek it, the better.

Understanding Testing and Diagnosis: Where to Start

Requesting additional accommodations often requires schools to allocate more resources and funding. Public schools operate within strict budgets and compliance frameworks—services are not automatically provided without documented need. Having an official diagnosis ensures your child qualifies for the appropriate support under the law. In other words, they're not going to give you anything for free without documentation.

Getting an evaluation for your child can feel like entering a maze without a map. There are acronyms, specialists, and stacks of paperwork—but behind all of that is something simple: the search for understanding. Testing doesn't define your child; it helps reveal how they learn and what kind of support they need to succeed.

Why Early Testing Matters

When a child struggles in school, adults often rush to fix the symptoms—extra tutoring, behavior charts, after-school programs—without understanding the cause. A proper evaluation gets to the root of the challenge. It identifies whether the issue stems from a learning disability, attention difference, sensory processing challenge, or another factor.

Testing provides the evidence that schools use to determine eligibility for special education or 504 accommodations under federal law. It also gives you, the parent, language and data to advocate more effectively. Once you understand how your child processes information, you can push for strategies that actually work.

If you have even a slight suspicion that your child may be on the autism spectrum, I cannot stress this enough: start the testing process before age eight. I found this out the hard way. He was now thirteen and trying to find a specialist for this age, but quickly, there was none. Many clinics have waitlists that can stretch for 6 months or more. A diagnosis opens the door to interventions that are most effective during the early developmental years, such as behavioral, speech, or occupational therapy.

The Two Main Paths to Evaluation

1. School-Based Evaluation (Through IDEA or Section 504)

Under the Individuals with Disabilities Education Act (IDEA), parents have the right to request a comprehensive evaluation if they suspect a disability that impacts learning. This process is free and conducted by the school's multidisciplinary team, which usually includes a psychologist, special educator, and other specialists.

Once you submit a written request, the school must respond within a specific timeframe usually 15 business days—and either obtain your consent to evaluate or explain why it denies the request. After consent, the evaluation must typically be completed within 60 days, though timelines vary by state.

The school uses the results to determine whether your child qualifies for an Individualized Education Program (IEP) or a Section 504 Plan. If the team concludes that the child does not qualify, you have the right to challenge that decision or seek an independent evaluation.

If you believe the school's evaluation is incomplete or inaccurate, you have the right to request an Independent Educational Evaluation (IEE) at public expense. If you make a request, the school district must pay an outside professional to conduct another assessment. You are not required to explain why you disagree with the initial results—simply state that you are exercising your right to an IEE under IDEA.

2. Private Evaluation

A licensed psychologist, neuropsychologist, or educational diagnostician can do a private evaluation. It's usually more detailed than a school evaluation and can cost anywhere from a few hundred to several thousand dollars, depending on location and provider.

While costly, private evaluations often provide more in-depth insight—especially if you suspect multiple factors (for example, ADHD combined with dyslexia or anxiety). If you share the private report with your school, they are required to consider its findings when determining eligibility or accommodations.

3. Pediatrician Evaluations (optional)

It's important to note that pediatricians, nor school-based evaluations, can confirm an accurate clinical diagnosis. Pediatricians rely on parent reports and school evaluations rather than on in-depth psychological testing when making diagnoses. For a correct diagnosis, you'll need to see a licensed private specialist, such as a child psychologist, psychiatrist, or neuropsychologist.

Here's what I learned through trial, error, and persistence:

1. **Start with your pediatrician.** Even though they can't provide a definitive diagnosis, they can give you a referral — and some clinics or insurance plans won't schedule you without one.

2. **Call multiple places at once.** Don't wait to hear back from just one office. Get on as many waitlists as possible; you can always cancel once you secure an appointment elsewhere.

3. **Ask about cancellation lists.** Some clinics offer call lists for families willing to come in on short notice if another patient cancels. Being placed on a cancellation list can save you months of waiting.

4. **Contact your local university or teaching hospital.** Many have developmental or psychology departments that offer assessments by graduate students under supervision—often at a lower cost and with shorter wait times.

5. **Check insurance coverage early.** Every insurance plan handles neuropsychological evaluations differently. While you're on the waitlist, request the billing codes from the institution's billing specialist—these are the codes they'll submit to your insurance company to verify coverage and payment. Do

some upfront legwork by calling your insurance provider to confirm whether those codes are covered. Knowing this information ahead of time helps you plan accordingly and avoid unexpected costs later.

What To Do While Waiting

While waiting for testing, keep detailed records of your child's school reports, teacher communications, behavior incidents, and academic performance. This documentation will be invaluable for your child's evaluation and can help professionals see patterns that aren't obvious from a single appointment. It also stands in for teachers who can't be there.

I started keeping a simple physical binder and a digital folder, divided into sections: school notes, medical updates, teacher emails, and observation logs. It became my most important resource through every meeting, every assessment, and every new professional who entered the picture-including the upfront paperwork to get on those waitlists. When you're advocating for your child, organized information is power.

Persistence Pays Off

There were days I felt like giving up — days when the process felt too bureaucratic, too slow, too heavy. But every call, every email, and every meeting moved us one step closer to answers. It wasn't easy, but it was necessary.

The truth is, you will have to advocate louder than you think you should. You will have to follow up repeatedly, ask tough questions, and sometimes remind professionals that your child isn't just another name on a list. You become your child's voice in systems that move slowly and lack simplicity.

And when that long-awaited evaluation day finally comes, it will all make sense. The hours spent researching, emailing, and pushing will have been worth it — because understanding your child's needs changes everything. It shifts you from reacting to behaviors to proactively supporting their growth.

Action Steps

1. Trust your gut. Don't wait.

- If something feels off—even if no one else sees it yet—act.

- You don't need permission to request an evaluation. Start early. The earlier the intervention, the better the outcome.

2. Request testing in writing.

- Ask your child's school for an evaluation in a formal letter. This formal request triggers legal timelines that require the school to respond.

- Use precise language: "I am formally requesting a comprehensive evaluation to determine whether my child qualifies for special education services under IDEA." See the Appendix for a template.

3. Know your evaluation options.

- School-Based Evaluation (free): Initiated through IDEA. The school team assesses and determines eligibility for an IEP or 504 Plan.

- Independent Educational Evaluation (IEE): If you disagree with the school's findings, you can request a second opinion—paid by the school district.

- Private Evaluation (paid): Deeper insights, but often costly. If shared, schools must consider the results.

- Pediatrician Referral: Start here for access to insurance-covered options, even if they can't give a complete diagnosis.

4. Call smart, call wide.

- Get on multiple waitlists at once.

- Ask for cancellation lists.

- Check local universities, teaching hospitals, or developmental clinics for faster, low-cost options.

5. Build your documentation binder.

- Keep everything: teacher notes, report cards, behavior logs, emails, and doctor visit summaries.

- Create both a physical binder and a digital folder—it's your advocacy portfolio.

6. Follow up… and follow up again.

- Systems are slow. People get busy. Keep checking in—by email, phone, whatever it takes.

- Use calendar reminders to track deadlines and progress.

7. Remember: Evidence = Leverage.

- A formal diagnosis gives you power. It opens legal rights, accommodations, and funding.

- You no longer have to "convince" people with emotion—you can show them proof.

CHAPTER 6

KNOW YOUR RIGHTS USE YOUR VOICE

With everything I had learned by that point, I knew my son's official diagnosis would finally unlock opportunities that had previously been out of reach. The previous school year had been so tumultuous—especially in our dealings with the school administration—that we decided to enroll him in a private school for seventh grade. But the transition back into public school for eighth grade was both necessary and strategic. As I mentioned in the previous chapter, the law requires public schools to provide disabled students with the accommodations and support they are entitled.

As a parent, you have necessary rights in the education system that help ensure your child receives the support they need to succeed. Knowing these rights empowers you to advocate effectively and navigate the processes schools provide.

Requesting Support and Evaluations

You can request meetings, evaluations, or assessments when your child needs extra support, including:

The Multi-Tiered System of Supports (MTSS) is how schools ensure every student gets the help they need to succeed, whether academically, behaviorally, or socially. Think of it like a ladder of support—students get more help only if they need it.

- **Tier 1:** Basic support for everyone. This tier is the regular classroom instruction with strategies that help most students succeed.

- **Tier 2:** Extra support for students who are struggling. For example, a small reading group or short social skills lessons.

- **Tier 3:** Intensive, personalized support for students with bigger challenges. This tier might include one-on-one instruction, counseling, or specialized interventions.

Imagine your child is having trouble with reading comprehension. In Tier 1, the classroom teacher implements strategies that support all students in better understanding texts. If your child still struggles, they may move to Tier 2, where they participate in a small reading group twice a week for targeted practice. If additional support is needed, Tier 3 offers individualized sessions with a reading specialist to address specific gaps. The foundation of MTSS—identifying what works early, adapting support over time, and working together as a team of educators, specialists, and parents to help your child succeed.

Schools use Functional Behavior Assessments (FBAs) to determine why a child behaves a certain way, especially when the behavior interferes with learning or daily life. Instead of punishing the behavior, an FBA identifies the cause so the school and family can provide appropriate support.

Imagine a child who frequently leaves their seat during class. An FBA might reveal that the child is getting up to avoid tasks that feel too hard or because the classroom is too noisy. Once the reason is apparent, the school can create a Behavior Intervention Plan (BIP), such as providing the child with a quiet space to work or breaking tasks into smaller steps, helping them succeed without punishment.

So how does it work? The school observes the child in different settings to see when and where the behavior occurs. They gather data on what triggers the behavior and what typically follows it. Evaluators interview teachers, parents, and sometimes the child to build a fuller picture. Then the team carefully analyzes the information to understand the function of the behavior—whether it's to gain attention, avoid a difficult task, or respond to sensory overload.

504 Plans are formal plans developed by schools to provide accommodations and support for students with disabilities who do not qualify for special education under the Individuals with Disabilities Education Act (IDEA) but still require assistance to participate in the general education environment fully.

504 Plans are part of Section 504 of the Rehabilitation Act of 1973, a federal civil rights law that protects individuals with disabilities from discrimination in programs that receive federal funding—including public schools.

Unlike an IEP, which focuses on specialized instruction, a 504 Plan ensures that a student has equal access to learning through accommodations such as:

- Extended time on tests or assignments

- Preferential seating

- Breaks during class

- Modified homework load

- Access to assistive technology

These supports level the playing field without altering academic expectations. The goal is to remove barriers that might prevent the student from learning or participating alongside their peers.

In short, an IEP changes what a student learns, while a 504 Plan changes how the student learns. Both serve to protect students' rights and promote school success. Also, this type of plan can follow your child through college.

Individualized Education Programs (IEPs) are a legally binding document developed for students who qualify for special education services under the Individuals with Disabilities Education Act (IDEA). It outlines a customized plan designed to meet the student's unique learning needs and ensure they receive a Free Appropriate Public Education (FAPE) in the Least Restrictive Environment (LRE).

An IEP includes specific details such as:

- The student's current academic and functional performance levels

- Measurable annual goals tailored to their needs

- Special education services and supports that the school will provide

- Accommodations and modifications for classroom instruction and testing

- Methods and timelines for tracking progress

The IEP is developed collaboratively by a team that typically includes the student's parents or guardians, teachers, school administrators, and specialists. This team meets at least once a year to review progress, but you can request follow-up meetings to adjust as needed. Do not skip these meetings or leave it to the administration and teachers to figure it out. Parents should attend to ensure their child receives the services they need.

The Legal Framework: Your Child's Rights

Federal laws, including the Individuals with Disabilities Education Act (IDEA) and Section 504 of the Rehabilitation Act, guarantee your child's right to accommodations, modifications, and specialized instruction. These laws prevent discrimination against people with disabilities and ensure equitable access to education.

- **Individuals with Disabilities Education Act (IDEA):** Provides eligible students with a Free Appropriate Public Education (FAPE) through an Individualized Education Program (IEP).

- **Section 504 of the Rehabilitation Act:** Prohibits discrimination based on disability in programs that receive federal funding, and mandates reasonable accommodations so students with disabilities can access education alongside peers.

- **Americans with Disabilities Act (ADA):** Broad nondiscrimination protections under public entities.

- **Office for Civil Rights (OCR):** The federal enforcement body that investigates complaints of discrimination in education. You can file a complaint within 180 calendar days of the discriminatory act (unless a waiver applies).

When Schools Don't Comply: What You Can Do

If you've had to work this hard-to-get learning supports in place for your child, chances are concerns will come up along the way. The key is to stay calm, informed, and strategic. When that time comes, you can escalate your concerns in stages:

Begin with informal discussions. If an issue arises, it's often best to talk with your child's teacher or another trusted staff member before jumping to conclusions. A respectful, brief email asking for clarification can help—many times, it's a simple misunderstanding. Keep in mind that not all teachers are thoroughly familiar with every child's accommodation, so a kind reminder can make a big difference.

If your child continues to struggle and you're having the same conversations without seeing progress, it's time to shift into formal communication. Submit a written request asking for a meeting to review your child's plan or request a new evaluation. Writing things down creates a clear record of your concerns and makes it easier to track the next steps.

If you believe discrimination or bias is playing a role, your school district likely has a grievance or complaint process in place. Filing a complaint can be stressful, but it's essential to document everything. Pay close attention to timelines and keep copies of any submissions you make.

When informal efforts and written requests don't lead to a resolution, you may need to explore legal options. Families can pursue mediation or due-process hearings when schools fail to respect their children's rights. These procedures exist to support fair outcomes under education law. Attorneys who specialize in education law can guide you through complex disputes involving IEPs, 504 plans, or disciplinary actions that may infringe on your child's rights.

You can also escalate your concerns by filing a federal complaint with the Office for Civil Rights

(OCR) or your state's education agency. Be sure to include all the necessary details—your identity, the name of the institution, the specific basis of discrimination, what happened, when it occurred, and why you believe the incident was discriminatory.

Actions to Take While the Complaint is Pending

Once the paperwork is submitted, it may feel like everything is out of your hands, but there's still plenty you can do. This period is about staying organized, informed, and proactive. Keep communication open, document every interaction, and focus on supporting your child's well-being while the process unfolds. Data is your anchor, document everything:

- Record dates, times, names, events, communications (emails, notes), missing support, discipline records, behavior logs, and academic data.

- Keep all copies of everything and create digital backups.

- Continue monitoring your child's progress and accommodations—don't assume the process ends there.

- Don't let retaliation go unnoticed—if it occurs (e.g., increased discipline for filing a complaint), document and report it.

- Ask for copies of behavior plans, suspensions, evaluation reports, IEPs/504 plans, and any correspondence. Make all requests in writing, keep copies, and create a file for reference.

CHAPTER 7

THE FOUR STEP SYSTEM THAT CHANGED EVERYTHING

There is a moment every parent advocate reaches, usually after a meeting that felt productive but changed nothing, when you realize the problem is not effort.

For me, that moment came after one too many conversations that ended with reassurance instead of action. I left meetings thinking we had alignment, only to discover weeks later that nothing had moved. The faces were familiar. The concerns were acknowledged. The language sounded right. But the outcome was always the same.

We were doing everything I thought "good parents" were supposed to do. We showed up. We explained. We advocated from the heart.

And still, nothing changed.

What I eventually learned is this: systems do not reward urgency; they respond to discipline. Not emotional discipline, but procedural discipline. A repeatable way of engaging that creates records, timelines, and accountability. Once we stopped relying on conversations to carry our child forward and started relying on structure, the dynamic shifted.

This chapter introduces the four-step process I now use every time I engage a school system:

Prepare > Document > Request > Follow Up

Not as a checklist. As a way of thinking.

Once I understood this sequence, advocacy stopped feeling like a constant fight. It began to feel intentional. Strategic. Grounded.

Step One: Prepare – Before You Ever Speak

Early on, I believed preparation meant knowing everything. I came into meetings armed with discipline notices, observations, and a running mental list of everything that had gone wrong. What I did not realize was that I was preparing to explain, not to decide.

Preparation is not about volume. It is about clarity and alignment.

Before every interaction now, I pause and ask what actually needs to happen next. Not what to vent about. Not what feels unfair. What decision needs to be made in this moment, and who has the authority to make it.

Before emails.

Before meetings.

Before casual conversations on the phone.

If I cannot name the outcome, I do not engage yet.

This shift mattered because I had learned the hard way that the system will happily let you talk.

It will nod. It will empathize. But it will not move unless you anchor the conversation to a decision point.

Preparation means deciding the lane before the system assigns you one. When I stopped walking into meetings ready to explain my child and started walking in ready to position a decision, the tone changed. The conversation changed. The results changed.

Preparation happens quietly.

Often alone.

And long before anyone else enters the room.

Step Two: Document – Because Memory Is Not a System

There was a time when I relied on memory. I trusted verbal commitments. I believed follow-through would happen because the conversation felt sincere.

That belief cost me time.

Documentation became necessary the first time I was told, "I don't recall agreeing to that," about something I remembered clearly. It became essential when patterns repeated and no one seemed to see them but me. I realized that without a written record, every concern reset to zero.

Documentation is not about being adversarial. It is about creating continuity.

Every system protects itself through records. If something is not written, it is optional. If it is written vaguely, it is easy to dismiss. When it is written clearly and consistently, it becomes harder to ignore.

My documentation includes dates, summaries, and follow-ups. It captures what was discussed, what was promised, and what did not happen. It avoids interpretation and focuses on facts. This record is not emotional. It does not need to be.

What documentation gave me was relief. I no longer had to remember everything. I no longer had to re-explain history. The record spoke for itself.

Step Three: Request – Precision Over Politeness

For a long time, I softened my asks. I thought being reasonable meant being vague. I worried that clarity would be perceived as aggression.

So I said things like, "I'm just concerned," or "I'd like some support," or "We need to talk about what's going on."

None of those were requests.

A request is not a narrative. It is not a complaint. It is not a feeling. A request is an action, assigned to someone, within a defined timeframe.

Learning this changed everything.

When I began stating my requests clearly, something interesting happened. Even when the answer was no, it was documented. And a documented no gave me direction. It narrowed the next step instead of stalling the process.

Clarity did not make me difficult.

It made me effective.

Once I stopped asking for understanding and started asking for action, the system had to respond.

Step Four: Follow Up - Where Most Advocacy Fails

Follow-up is where strategy becomes visible. It used to feel uncomfortable. I worried about being seen as persistent or pushy. What I eventually realized is that follow-up is not personal. It is procedural.

Follow-up is how systems operate. Every follow-up I send references the record. It confirms what was completed, clarifies what was not, or escalates when needed. There is no emotion attached to it. Just continuity.

This step is where advocacy stops relying on goodwill and starts relying on accountability.

When you follow up consistently, you become predictable. The system learns that commitments matter because someone is tracking them. Over time, behavior shifts. Not because you demanded it, but because the structure required it.

Action Step

This process works when you apply it consistently—not perfectly. The goal isn't flawless execution; it's stability and follow-through.

If you have a meeting coming up:

- Identify one clear decision needed during that meeting.

- Write it down before you walk in. If the decision doesn't get made, a follow-up meeting is necessary.

If a request is already in progress:

- Send a short follow-up to confirm status: what was the agreement, what's already in place, and what's still outstanding.

- Ask directly for the next action, the owner, and the timeline.

During and after every interaction:

- Document the discussion, the commitments made, and what didn't happen.

- Put requests in writing with clear, specific language—avoid vague asks.

- Follow up until the loop is closed, not until the meeting ends.

Let the process carry the weight, not you. When expectations, decisions, and next steps live on paper, momentum becomes easier to maintain—and harder to ignore.

This is not about being louder. It is about being anchored. This is how advocacy becomes sustainable, trackable, and keeps you grounded instead of exhausted.

CHAPTER 8

BUILDING A SCHOOL TEAM THAT WORKS

Supporting your child effectively requires collaboration—and that means building a strong team of educators, specialists, and administrators who understand your child's needs. Early in my journey advocating for my son, I wasn't always confident in these meetings; I often let the school staff lead the conversation, hoping they would offer services I didn't know about. I was so wrong.

Over time, I realized the power of preparation. Now, I approach every meeting backed with documentation, specific examples, and a structured plan. This preparation allows me to own the room, ensuring that everyone is aligned around clear, measurable goals and shared accountability. By taking the lead, I ensure that each team member understands their role in supporting my son's success and that our collective efforts focus on tangible outcomes.

When it comes to advocating for your child in IEP or 504 meetings, preparation is your superpower. You don't need to be an expert—but you do need to be informed, organized, and intentional. Here's how to approach the process with clarity and confidence at every stage:

Your work begins before the meeting ever starts. These steps ensure your voice is centered and that the school team walks in with a clearer understanding of your child beyond the data.

- Bring Data and Examples: Remember when I said document, document, document? Well, this is your time to show and tell. Come prepared with recent grades, missing assignments, teacher notes, and observations from home. Concrete examples make it easier to connect your child's daily experiences to their support needs.

When you're in the room—virtual or otherwise—clarity is key. These are powerful ways to ensure the plan is specific, practical, and actionable.

- Ask for Measurable, Skill-Based Goals: Goals should be specific and trackable—not vague promises. For example:

  - "By the end of the semester, [Student] will complete 90% of assignments on time with adult check-ins and organizational support."

  - "Given explicit instruction and visual aids, [Student] will demonstrate understanding of [specific concept] in [subject] with 80% accuracy."

  - "When feeling anxious or overwhelmed, [Student] will use one self-regulation strategy (e.g., break, deep breathing, check-in with staff) in 4 out of 5 observed opportunities."

- Clarify Accountability: Identify who is responsible for implementing each accommodation. For example, who ensures your child receives a quiet space for tests or extended time for assignments? Each item should have a clear point of contact.

• Request a Mid-Semester Review: Don't wait until the next annual or semiannual meeting. Ask for a progress review midway through the semester to assess whether supports are working.

The meeting may be over, but your role continues. Here's how to make sure agreements don't get lost in the shuffle.

• Hold the School Accountable: Follow up in writing to confirm agreed-upon actions, responsibilities, and timelines.

- Don't Hesitate to Request Addendum Meetings: If something isn't working, you have the right to call another meeting to adjust the plan. Again, you don't need to wait for the following scheduled review.

- Don't Assume Every Teacher Has Read the IEP or 504: Communicate directly with teachers—especially new ones or substitutes—to ensure they understand your child's accommodations and how to implement them.

Reread this one.

And If You Need to Escalate…

Sometimes, despite your best efforts, things still fall through the cracks. If others ignore your concerns or fail to meet your child's needs, you still have power. You can file a grievance, request mediation, or escalate to your district's special education office or even the Office for Civil Rights.

And if that still doesn't work—know this: you are allowed to ask for help. Educational advocates, disability rights organizations, and attorneys who specialize in education law are all available to support you. You don't have to figure this out alone.

Because when it comes to your child's future, silence isn't an option—and persistence is a plan.

Finally, advocating for your child is not a one-time event—it's an ongoing journey that requires persistence, preparation, and heart. While the systems in place may be complex and, at times, discouraging, your voice matters. You are the expert on your child, and your insights are essential to building the kind of educational support they deserve. When meetings feel overwhelming, or outcomes feel uncertain, remember: you are not just attending for the sake of process—you're showing up to protect your child's right to learn, grow, and thrive. Keep showing up. Keep asking questions. Keep pushing forward.

Action Step

Start building a dedicated binder (or cloud folder) to organize all documents related to your child's education. Include evaluations, progress reports, IEPs/504 Plans, teacher emails, behavior logs, meeting notes, and any communication with the school. Use tabs or folders to separate by topic or date. Having everything in one place makes it easier to advocate clearly, follow up efficiently, and respond confidently when unexpected issues arise.

CHAPTER 9

ADVOCACY IN ACTION

Effective advocacy is about more than knowing the laws or attending meetings—it's about how you communicate, build relationships, and remain focused on your child's success. Even when meetings feel emotional, a strategic approach helps you get heard and secure the support your child needs.

It's also about truly knowing your child. For example, my son would start the school year strong, but once he settled in, his behavior would often go off track. Understanding these patterns allows you, as a parent, to approach the year strategically—armed with preparation, insight, and a dedicated team on your side.

I cannot emphasize enough how important it is for you to make sure every teacher knows who you are and sees that you are both consistent and deeply engaged. Show them that you're not there to criticize or complicate their work—you're there to partner with them. When educators understand that you're on their team, it not only makes their job easier but also encourages them to keep you informed without you having to chase updates.

And when you build relationships grounded in transparency, shared data, and mutual responsibility, something powerful happens you stop feeling like you're battling the system alone and instead begin leading a team that is actively working alongside you for your child's success.

Advocacy is not a one-time effort; it is an ongoing process. And sometimes it feels like a full-time job. Once accommodations and supports are in place, you must maintain momentum to ensure schools implement them consistently and adapt them to your child's evolving needs. By consistently applying these strategies, you transform from a reactive parent into a proactive advocate.

Reach Out Early and Often

Don't wait for a crisis or the end of the grading period to contact teachers or administrators. Regular check-ins allow you to address minor issues before they escalate into bigger problems. Early communication demonstrates your engagement and gives the school time to implement supports effectively.

Schedule frequent, brief check-ins with teachers, counselors, and other staff members. Weekly or biweekly updates, even via email, help you stay informed about your child's academic performance, behavior, and emotional well-being. These check-ins help you identify challenges early and address them before they become bigger issues.

Monitor your child's progress regularly. Review homework, check grades, and talk with teachers about classroom performance and behavior. Luckily, my son's school posts grades almost daily. Although he lives with his dad full-time, I remain deeply involved. I check in every day to catch any missing assignments—or to celebrate that A+ he "forgot" to mention during the usual brief, one-word conversations that come with parenting a teenager. Being informed allows you to notice patterns, celebrate successes, and address challenges in real-time.

Use the goals established in your child's IEP or 504 plan as your roadmap. Track progress using grades, completed assignments, behavioral observations, and teacher feedback. Document both successes and areas where support may be falling short. Mid-semester reviews are an excellent opportunity to adjust strategies and observe progress.

Meetings can become emotional, but the most effective advocates stay calm and professional.

Bring notes if you need to, so you can stay organized and clearly communicate your thoughts and requests. Focus on your child's needs rather than personalities or frustrations. Even when challenges arise, maintain a calm, solution-focused approach.

Avoid letting frustration or emotion dominate discussions. Focus on objective data, measurable outcomes, and actionable solutions. This approach strengthens your credibility and helps build collaborative relationships with educators.

If I haven't said it enough already, you're going to hear it again: when a strategy or accommodation isn't working, don't wait for the following annual review—request an addendum meeting. Be specific about what's not effective and come prepared with possible alternatives. Staying flexible and proactive ensures your child's plan continues to evolve as their needs change.

Acknowledging small victories reinforces your child's confidence and demonstrates to the school that supports are producing results. Recognize academic successes, improvements in behavior, and any progress toward social or emotional goals.

Laws, policies, and best practices change over time. Stay up to date on educational rights, intervention strategies, and available resources. The more informed you are, the more vigorous advocate you can be.

When Meetings Go Off Track

Sometimes, despite your best preparation, a meeting can go badly. Emotions rise, communication breaks down, or you leave feeling unheard and defeated. It happens—and it doesn't mean you've failed. It means you're fighting for something that matters. If a meeting doesn't go well, take a pause, breathe, and reflect. Then, follow up in writing.

Summarize what was said, clarify misunderstandings, and restate your concerns and expectations. A respectful, well-documented follow-up email can reset the tone, establish accountability, and open the door for more productive dialogue. And if your emotions rise during the meeting—which is entirely normal—acknowledge it without apology, but steer the conversation back to your child's needs. It's okay to say: "I'm feeling overwhelmed right now because I want to make sure my child gets what they need. Can we take a quick pause or come back to this point after we review the data?" You don't have to be perfect to be effective—you just have to stay rooted in your purpose.

Action Step

Prepare a simple email template you can use after any school meeting, especially after a difficult one. Build your template with sections that summarize the discussion, clarify next steps, capture corrections, and define what comes next. This format not only documents your concerns but helps re-establish clarity, professionalism, and shared accountability.

____

____

____

____

____

CHAPTER 10

RAISING A SELF-ADVOCATE

When my son first started receiving services, I did most of the talking. I sat in meetings, wrote emails, and explained his needs in detail. But as he grew older, I began to realize something important: the best advocate for him wasn't me—it was himself. My job was to give him the tools, language, and confidence to use his own voice.

He's now fifteen and in ninth grade, so this process is a bit easier now that he's older—but it can be more challenging with younger children. Self-advocacy doesn't develop overnight. We've been preparing him since he was young, guiding him to speak for himself when we aren't present. It requires patience, modeling, and age-appropriate support. Yet when children learn to use their voices, they gain confidence, independence, and a genuine sense of ownership over their education and well-being.

This chapter is about helping your child step into their own power. Advocacy isn't just a parent's role—it's a lifelong skill your child can carry into every space they enter.

To help your child develop a strong sense of identity and self-advocacy, it's important to talk openly about their diagnosis and involve them in understanding their learning needs. This section offers practical steps for building your child's confidence, helping them use their voice, and preparing them to take ownership of their support—now and in the future.

1. Talking About Disability Openly

Many parents, including us, hesitate to talk about diagnoses or labels, fearing it might discourage their child. We never told our son of his diagnosis or spoke the ADHD terms around him because we didn't want him to use it as an excuse for his behavior in his younger years. We told him he gets extra support to help him, never the why behind it. Kids know when we're hiding something. When we avoid the topic, they fill in the blanks with self-blame.

It wasn't until I was pushing for the evaluation that he began to ask questions. I suddenly felt so guilty for keeping it from him all that time. When you discuss your child's diagnosis, frame it as a difference, not a deficiency. Say, "Your brain works in a way that makes reading harder, but it also helps you notice patterns other people miss." or "You need more time for writing, but you're amazing at explaining ideas out loud."

Language matters. It shapes how your child sees themselves. Pride and understanding are antidotes to shame.

2.   Start Early, Even in Small Ways

For younger children, self-advocacy begins with awareness. Help them identify when something feels challenging or overwhelming and encourage them to express that to you or a trusted adult. Phrases like "I need help," "This is too loud," or "Can I take a break?" are the building blocks of self-advocacy.

Model what it looks like to communicate calmly and respectfully. When you talk to teachers or staff, let your child observe how you describe challenges and solutions—they're learning from your example.

3. Empower Older Students to Participate

As children enter middle and high school, they should begin taking a more active role in their own educational planning. Encourage them to attend IEP or 504 meetings, even if only for part of the session, to share what's working, what's not, and what helps them succeed.

Before meetings, help them prepare talking points such as:

- "I focus better when I can move around."

- "I get overwhelmed when I have too many instructions at once."

- "Having extra time on tests helps me think clearly."

This form of empowerment builds self-awareness and reinforces the idea that their opinions matter.

Some kids aren't comfortable talking in front of adults—and that's okay. Advocacy doesn't have to look one way. They can:

- Write a letter to be read aloud in the meeting.

- Record a short video sharing their thoughts.

- Create a list of goals or concerns for you to present.

The key is that they're included, not left out. Each small step builds confidence for the next.

4.   Foster Responsibility and Accountability

Empowerment also means accountability. Encourage your child to track their own assignments, monitor grades, and practice using tools that support them (planners, reminders, or visual aids). It teaches independence and helps them transition those advocacy skills beyond the classroom.

We began putting this into practice with him around sixth or seventh grade, helping him understand that he had a responsibility in making these efforts successful—it wasn't just his parents nagging or reminding him. By involving him in setting goals, tracking his progress, and communicating with teachers, he gradually learned to take ownership of his learning and behavior. This shift not only empowered him to advocate for his own needs but also strengthened his confidence and independence, showing him that his voice truly matters in shaping his education and daily life.

5.   Reframe Challenges as Strengths

Children often internalize their struggles as personal failures. As parents, we can shift that narrative by highlighting their resilience, creativity, and persistence. Remind them that needing support doesn't mean they're incapable—it means they're learning how to navigate the world in a way that works best for them.

6.   Create Safe Spaces for Expression

At home, create an environment where your child feels comfortable sharing their frustrations and victories. Listen without judgment, validate their feelings, and brainstorm solutions together. The more supported they feel at home, the more confident they'll be advocating for themselves in school.

Empowering your child to use their voice is one of the greatest gifts you can give them. It turns advocacy from something done for them into something done with them. Over time, children learn that their perspective has value, their needs deserve respect, and their voice can create change— not just in school, but in every part of their life.

The ultimate goal of advocacy is independence. Whether your child goes to college, enters the workforce, or follows a different path, they'll need to explain what they need to succeed. By teaching them to understand and express their needs early, you're setting them up for a lifetime of self-empowerment.

When my son learned to speak for himself, it wasn't just about school. It was about confidence, pride, and knowing that his differences were not barriers—they were part of his story.

Action Step

Sit down with your child this week and ask them to describe one thing that feels hard at school and one thing that helps them. Write down their answers, and with their permission, include them in your subsequent communication with their teacher or support team. Including them in this way not only validates their experience but also actively involves them in shaping the supports that will help them succeed.

CHAPTER 11

LIVING THE PLAN AT HOME AND SCHOOL

Once meetings end and plans are in writing, many parents feel a mix of relief and uncertainty. The question becomes: Now what? What does daily life look like with all of these accommodations? How do I support my child from home? How do we build routines that actually help?

The truth is, the IEP or 504 is just the beginning—it's the framework. The real progress happens in the ordinary, daily moments. It's in the way we start mornings, how we support homework time, and how we build rhythms that honor our child's needs without overwhelming ourselves.

Mornings can make or break a day. For kids with executive functioning challenges, transitions, time pressure, and sensory overload can be intense. Building a calm, predictable routine can ease anxiety and set the tone.

Tips For Smoother Mornings:

- Visual schedules: Use pictures or checklists so your child can follow steps independently (e.g., get dressed, brush teeth, eat breakfast, pack a bag).

- Prep the night before: Lay out clothes, pack backpacks, and review any to-dos. Doing things in advance reduces stress for everyone.

- Set multiple alarms: Use different tones or locations to help your child transition between tasks (invaluable for kids with ADHD).

- Create a calm zone: If mornings are overwhelming, designate a quiet spot where your child can regulate with a fidget, calming music, or a few minutes of silence.

Homework can trigger frustration, primarily if your child associates it with struggle or past failures. With accommodations in place, you support rather than rescue and help your child use the tools available to them.

At-home Strategies:

• Create a distraction-free space: Keep the environment consistent and clutter-free. Use noise-canceling headphones or quiet playlists if needed.

• Break tasks into chunks: Even if the teacher didn't modify the homework, you can. Help your child tackle 10 minutes at a time with short breaks.

• Use timers and visuals: Time management tools like timers, checklists, or "first/then" boards help keep things on track without you having to nag.

- Check in, but don't hover: Sit nearby but let them lead. If they get stuck, coach them to use their accommodations ("What's your strategy for this?") instead of stepping in immediately.

After school is often when fatigue hits, and it's tempting to drop structure—but consistency helps kids decompress and prepare for the next day. Routine elements to consider:

- Unwind first: Give 30–60 minutes of free time after school before diving into tasks.

- Snack + talk: Food + low-pressure conversation helps build connection and creates space to process their day.

- Homework + check-ins: Once they're regulated, start on homework with an agreed-upon routine.

- Preview the next day: Go over any materials, forms, or changes so your child feels prepared—not surprised.

With supports in place at school, your role shifts to coaching independence—helping your child practice self-awareness and responsibility in safe, supported ways. What this looks like:

- Encourage your child to check their own backpack and planner.

- Have them email a teacher (with your help) when something's unclear.

- Involve them in setting routines: "What time should homework start?" "How will you remember your water bottle?"

- Give praise for effort, not just results: "I saw how you kept trying even when that was hard."

Even with a great plan, there will be off days. Homework might get missed. Meltdowns might happen. Plans will fall apart. That doesn't mean the plan isn't working. It means your child is human—and so are you. When days go sideways:

- Lead with connection: "That was a tough day. I'm proud of how you got through it."

- Reset, don't react: Start fresh the next day. No one learns well through shame or punishment.

- Review the plan: If a pattern continues, it may be time for an adjustment—not just more discipline.

Action Step

Build your home-based success system by taking 20 minutes this week to create a home routine checklist. Include a morning schedule, after-school routine, and homework time plan. Involve your child in the process—they'll be more likely to follow a routine they helped design. Post it in a visible spot and treat it like a living document you can tweak as needed.

____

____

____

____

____

____

____

CHAPTER 12

GRACE FOR THE JOURNEY

If there's one part of this journey we don't talk about enough, it's the emotional toll it takes on us as parents. When I think back on the early days of Son's journey, what stands out most isn't the paperwork or the meetings—it's the emotions. The fear. The guilt.

Advocacy is deeply personal work that touches every part of who you are. You're not only fighting for your child's education; you're constantly questioning yourself, managing the weight of guilt, and trying to pour from a cup that's already half empty.

I used to think if I just worked harder, stayed up later, researched more, or sent one more email, things would finally click into place. But it is not a sprint, it's a marathon. And without balance, even the strongest parents can find themselves emotionally drained.

Grief and Guilt

When you first realize your child learns or experiences the world differently, it can feel like your expectations have been rewritten. Even when the diagnosis brings relief—finally having answers—it can also bring grief. You may grieve the imagined path you thought your child would take or, like me, the anguish of all he had been through.

That's okay. Grief doesn't mean you love your child any less or that any of it is your fault. It means you're adjusting to a new understanding of who they are and what they need.

Acceptance doesn't happen overnight. It's a process of letting go of comparison and learning to see your child not through the lens of what's missing, but through what makes them. Their progress might not fit the world's timeline, but it's still progress.

And then there's guilt. Guilt shows up in quiet ways. It whispers in your ear at night, replaying moments when you lost your patience or missed another email from the school. It questions every decision—Should I have pushed harder? Should I have known sooner? Should I have done more?

I've felt it all. The guilt of wondering if I'm doing too much or not enough. The guilt of seeing my child struggle and not having an instant fix. The guilt of needing a break but feeling selfish for wanting one. And don't even get me started on the defeat I felt when I had to put my ego aside and he went to live with his father. I felt like a complete failure—heartbroken, conflicted, and guilty for the small, whispered sense of relief that came with finally having help.

But here's the truth: guilt doesn't serve your child; grace does. You're human. You're learning a system that even professionals struggle to navigate, while also parenting, working, and managing life. None of us start this journey with a roadmap. We learn as we go. What matters is that you keep showing up. Every meeting you attend, every form you fill out, every late-night email you send—it all matters. Perfection isn't required. Presence is.

You can't control every outcome, but you can control how you care for yourself through it. When guilt starts to creep in, pause and remind yourself of what you are doing. You're showing up. You're learning. You're advocating for your child in ways that many parents never have to. That's not failure, that's love in action.

The Reality of Burnout

There comes a point when you realize that advocating for your child can feel like a job in itself, and sometimes, it really is. Between managing paperwork, scheduling evaluations, emailing teachers, and emotionally supporting your child, it can start to feel like your own needs no longer matter.

Burnout doesn't happen all at once. It builds slowly, in the small moments when you push through exhaustion, convince yourself you can't stop, and ignore the signs that you need rest. You might find yourself more irritable, less patient, or simply numb to the process.

I remember a season when I was so deep in the process that I barely recognized myself. My days revolved around research, meetings, and planning. My evenings were spent catching up on work I missed while advocating. My weekends were filled with recovery from the emotional hangover of yet another tense meeting. I was functioning—but I wasn't okay.

If you're reading this and feeling that way, know this: taking care of yourself is part of the advocacy process. You can't pour into your child's growth from an empty cup. Rest isn't a reward, it's a requirement.

Start small. Step away from the constant research. Give yourself permission to turn off the advocacy brain for an evening. Go for a walk, listen to music that soothes your soul, call a friend who makes you laugh. Even five minutes of breathing room can reset your spirit.

Finding Support

The most powerful shift in my journey came when I stopped trying to do it all alone. While his dad has always been just as heavily involved post-divorce, deciding that our Son would live with him full-time was one of the hardest choices I've ever made. As a mother, I carried so much guilt and shame—feeling like I should've been able to handle everything myself. It wasn't that I wanted to do it all; I just wanted to fix it all. But no amount of effort could change the truth that I was exhausted and needed help.

For a long time, I believed no one could truly understand what I was going through unless they were living it too—and in some ways, that was true. But over time, I realized there were people who genuinely wanted to help; they just didn't know how until I let them in.

Find your people. Join local or online parent advocacy groups—places like Understood.org or Facebook communities for parents of neurodiverse children. Some counties have groups as well. These spaces are full of others who speak the same "language" of accommodations, evaluations, and emotional exhaustion. Hearing "me too" from another parent can instantly lift a weight off your shoulders.

Don't be afraid to ask for help from friends and family. Sometimes, that means asking them to pick up your child so you can have an hour to yourself. Other times, it's simply asking someone to listen without judgment. The more open you are about your struggles, the less power isolation has over you.

You might also find strength in professional support—therapy, parent coaching, or counseling can help you process the emotions that advocacy stirs up. It's not weakness; it's wisdom. Having a space to cry, vent, or reflect helps you stay steady for the long haul.

Reconnecting with Joy

It's easy to get so focused on what's wrong that we forget what's right. Between behavioral reports and academic meetings, joy can feel like something you have to schedule. But our children, and we, deserve moments of light.

Celebrate small wins. Maybe your child remembered to turn in an assignment or managed a tough day without a meltdown. Maybe you handled a meeting with more confidence than last time. Those victories matter. They remind you that progress is happening, even if it's not always visible.

I began to notice that the more I celebrated joy, the more my Son did, too. When I replace constant correction with genuine acknowledgment of effort, his confidence grows—

and so does mine. Joy doesn't erase struggle, but it makes the journey more bearable.

Giving Yourself Permission to Be Enough

This chapter isn't about perfection—it's about permission. Permission to rest. Permission to feel angry, tired, or uncertain. Permission to laugh in the middle of the mess. Permission to say, "I'm doing my best, and that's enough for today."

Because you are enough. The fact that you're reading this, learning, and trying, means you've already done something extraordinary. You've chosen to show up, again and again, in a system that often makes parents feel small. That's not weakness—it's resilience.

You are your child's anchor, but you also deserve to float sometimes. To breathe. To heal. Advocacy isn't just about changing systems—it's about protecting your own light so you can keep showing up.

So, as you continue on this journey, remember: your strength isn't measured by how much you do—it's measured by how deeply you love, and how gently you care for yourself along the way.

Action Step

Take five minutes today to reflect—not on what still needs to be done, but on what you've already survived and accomplished. Write down three ways you've shown up for your child in the past month, no matter how small they may seem. Then, write down one thing you will do for yourself this week—something that nourishes your energy or brings you joy. Advocacy isn't just about pushing forward—it's about pausing, too. You matter in this journey, and so does your healing.

CONCLUSION

YOU ARE THE CONSTANT

You've made it through a significant turning point—both in my story and, I hope, in your own. If you're here, you're likely navigating the journey of advocating for your child, searching for answers, or feeling overwhelmed by systems that weren't built with your child in mind. So let's turn everything we've just covered into concrete, empowering action steps.

1. Start the Evaluation Process—Don't Wait

If your gut is telling you something isn't right, listen. You do not need permission to begin advocating. Whether it's requesting a formal evaluation through the school or scheduling a private assessment, early testing matters. The sooner you have clarity, the sooner you can begin pushing for meaningful support.

2. Document Everything

Create a system for collecting data—emails, behavior logs, academic progress, evaluations, and communication with staff. Keep digital folders and hard copies. This paper trail becomes your evidence, your timeline, and your power when advocating through meetings, complaints, or legal steps.

3. Get to Know the Tools: IEP, 504, FBA, MTSS

Each tool is different, but together they form a map of support. Learn the difference between an IEP and a 504 Plan. Know when to ask for a Functional Behavior Assessment (FBA) or how MTSS can offer earlier interventions. You don't have to be an expert overnight, but understanding the basics will help you make more informed decisions—and hold schools accountable.

4. Use Your Rights Strategically

Federal law protects your child. IDEA, Section 504, and the ADA all exist for a reason. If your school is not meeting its legal obligations, start with respectful conversations, then move to formal written requests. If needed, escalate to your district, state education agency, or the Office for Civil Rights. Don't let fear stop you from using the protections your child is entitled to.

5. Build a Support Team

You don't have to do this alone. Whether it's a trusted teacher, a special education advocate, a parent support group, or legal counsel—surround yourself with people who understand the system and will stand with you when it gets hard.

6. Turning Strategy Into Impact

Advocacy in action is where strategy meets consistency—how you communicate, show up, and stay focused determines whether support actually happens. When you lead with clarity and preparation, you build trust, reinforce accountability, and turn intention into real impact.

7. Building Voice and Confidence

Raising a self-advocate means gradually transferring knowledge, confidence, and voice to your child so they can speak up for their own needs. Through guidance and trust, they learn to understand how they learn, recognize their strengths, and carry that advocacy beyond the classroom.

8. From Paper to Everyday Practice

Living the plan means ensuring that what's written on paper is consistently applied in real life—at school and at home. When support is reinforced daily and everyone stays aligned, plans become lived experiences that drive meaningful, lasting growth.

9. Take Care of Yourself, Too

Advocating is emotionally exhausting work. You are your child's advocate, yes—but you're also their emotional anchor. Make time to rest, process, and recharge. Advocacy is a marathon, not a sprint.

Lastly, you are no longer just reacting to problems. You're creating a plan. You're driving the conversation. Through your actions, you're shaping a future where your child is fully seen, understood, and supported. And that changes everything.

If you haven't already, now is the time to make your list, schedule those calls, send that email, or start building that binder. It doesn't have to be perfect—it just has to begin.

There will come a moment—maybe late at night after a long meeting, or quietly while watching your child solve a problem in their own unique way—when it hits you: You've come so far. And so has your child.

What began as a confusing, overwhelming, and sometimes heartbreaking journey has slowly become a path paved with strength, knowledge, and advocacy. Not because the system suddenly became easier, but because you became more powerful within it.

You've learned the acronyms. You've shown up at meetings. You've asked hard questions. You've found your voice, and more importantly, you've helped your child begin to find theirs, too. That's no small feat.

As you continue forward through new schools, changing teachers, and evolving needs, you carry clarity, courage, and the confidence to keep going.

Your child may not always follow the traditional path. Their story may include unexpected turns and delayed milestones. But progress isn't always linear, and success isn't one-size-fits-all. The goal has never been perfection—it's been connection, advocacy, and a life where your child feels seen, supported, and celebrated.

Remember, this work is never about doing it all. It's about doing what matters most: showing up with love, knowledge, and resilience. You don't have to have every answer. You just have to stay in the room.

You are the expert on your child. You are their advocate. Their translator. Their mirror. Their safe place.

And as long as you keep believing in their potential, you're already helping them succeed.

The story doesn't end here—it's just the

beginning of a new chapter. One where your child

knows they are not broken or behind. They are

precisely who they're supposed to be."

And you? You are precisely the parent they need.

REFERENCE

Americans with Disabilities Act of 1990, 42 U.S.C. § 12101.

Baumer, N., & Frueh, J. (2021). What is neurodiversity? Harvard Health Publishing. https://www.health.harvard.edu/blog/what-is-neurodiversity-202111232645

Columbia Teachers College. (2021). Dual enrollment and AP access study.

Cornell Health. (2021). Study breaks and stress busters.

Individuals with Disabilities Education Act, 20 U.S.C. § 1400 (2004). §300.301–300.309.

Individuals with Disabilities Education Act, 20 U.S.C. § 1400 (2004). §300.301–300.311.

Individuals with Disabilities Education Act, 20 U.S.C. § 1400 (2004). §300.321–300.324.

Individuals with Disabilities Education Act, 20 U.S.C. § 1400 (2004). §300.500–300.518.

Individuals with Disabilities Education Act, 20 U.S.C. § 1400 (2004). §300.530.

Mainsbridge, C., et al. (2019). Prolonged sitting and attention outcomes.

National Alliance on Mental Illness. (2022). Parent resilience and support resources.

National Parent Center on Transition and Employment. (2023). Life after high school toolkit.

Pontifex, M. B., et al. (2021). Research on movement and cognitive performance.

Section 504 of the Rehabilitation Act of 1973, 29 U.S.C. § 794.

Singer, J. (1998). Odd people in: The birth of community amongst people on the autism spectrum. Habilitant.

U.S. Commission on Civil Rights. (2019). Beyond suspensions: Examining discipline and disability in schools.

U.S. Department of Education. (2022). Office for Civil Rights discipline data.

U.S. Department of Education. (2022). Parent and educator guide to IDEA evaluations.

U.S. Department of Education. (2022). Parent and educator guide to IEP teams.

U.S. Department of Education, Office for Civil Rights. (2022). Civil Rights Data Collection: Discipline, restraint, and seclusion.

U.S. Department of Education. (2023). Parent Guide to Special Education Terms

U.S. Department of Education. (2023). Transition planning guide for students with disabilities.

Understood.org. (2023). Coping with the emotional side of advocacy.

Understood.org. (2023). How to talk with schools about your child's needs.

Understood.org. (2023). Signs of learning differences and when to request an evaluation.

Understood.org. (2023). When you suspect your child may have a learning difference.

Webster, C. A., et al. (2015). Effects of classroom physical activity on focus and engagement. Journal of Physical Activity & Health.

WrightsLaw. (2023). Advocacy strategies and communication tips.

WrightsLaw. (2023). Effective communication with schools.

WrightsLaw. (2023). Postsecondary options and transition planning.

WrightsLaw. (2023). Self-care for advocates and families.

WrightsLaw. (2023). Understanding evaluations, tests, and assessments.

WrightsLaw. (2023). Understanding IEPs, 504s, and the language of special education.

APPENDIX A

RESOURCES AND TEMPLATES FOR PARENTS

Advocacy is emotional, exhausting, and at times confusing, but it's also a skill that grows stronger with the right tools and support. In this section, you'll find a collection of resources and customizable templates to support you every step of the way—from requesting evaluations to preparing for school meetings and tracking progress at home. These templates are starting points—feel free to adapt them to your voice, your child's needs, and your school's culture.

They guide you to communicate confidently with schools, document your child's needs, and understand your rights. These are the same kinds of tools that helped me learn how to speak the system's language. As you prepare to take action on everything you've learned in this book, it's important to remember that you don't have to start from scratch or sound like a lawyer to be effective. Think of this as your personal toolkit—practical, proven, and ready when you are.

Key Websites & Learning Resources

Parent Advocacy & Education Rights

- **Understood.org** — Guides, templates, and expert advice for parents of neurodiverse children.

- **Wright's Law** — Legal explanations, sample letters, and parent rights under IDEA and Section 504. https://wrightslaw.com/

- **ADDitude Magazine** — Articles, webinars, and tools for parenting children with ADHD and related conditions. https://www.additudemag.com/

- **U.S. Department of Education, Office for Civil Rights** — For filing discrimination or 504/IDEA complaints. https://www.ed.gov/laws-and-policy/civil-rights-laws/file-complaint

- **Center for Parent Information & Resources** — State-by-state listings of parent training and advocacy centers. https://www.parentcenterhub.org/

- **Council of Parent Attorneys and Advocates (COPAA)** — National nonprofit supporting parents with legal guidance and advocacy resources. https://www.copaa.org/

- **CHADD (Children and Adults with Attention-Deficit/Hyperactivity Disorder)** — Evidence-based information, training, and local chapter support groups. https://chadd.org/

- **Autism Speaks Toolkits** — Practical guides for IEP meetings, school transitions, and community support. https://www.autismspeaks.org/autism-speaks-tool-kits

Learning Support Tools

- **Understood.org's School Communication Templates -** https://www.understood.org/en/topics/parent-teacher-conferences

- **Google Keep or Notion** — Tools for organizing documentation, meeting notes, and reminders.

- **ADDitude's Free Downloadables** — Printable planners, homework systems, and behavior charts. https://www.additudemag.com/category/parenting-adhd-kids/download-parents/

Advocacy & Organization Tools

Parent Documentation Binder Setup

Create sections for:

1.Evaluations & Reports

2.504/IEP Documents

3.Teacher Communication

4.Behavioral/Disciplinary Records

5.Medical or Clinical Updates

6.Notes from Meetings

7.Progress Data

Digital Tools

• Google Drive or Dropbox: For saving and sharing official documents.

• **ColorNote or Notion:** For quick notes after meetings or calls.

• **Canva:** Create a visual "Profile Sheet" about your child's strengths, triggers, and best supports to give to teachers at the start of the year.

Template Letters & Emails

1. Sample Letter: Request for Learning Support or Evaluation

Subject: Request for Evaluation to Determine Educational Supports for [Child's Name]

Dear [Principal's Name or School Counselor's Name],

I am writing to formally request an evaluation for my child, [Child's Name], who is in [Grade/Class] at [School Name]. I have observed ongoing challenges with [briefly describe — e.g., attention, reading, behavior, organization, or emotional regulation] that appear to impact [his/her/their] learning and classroom performance.

Under the Individuals with Disabilities Education Act (IDEA) and Section 504 of the Rehabilitation Act, I am requesting that the school conduct a comprehensive evaluation to determine whether my child qualifies for accommodations or specialized services.

Please confirm in writing that my request has been received and share the following steps, including the evaluation timeline and any forms I need to complete.

Thank you for your attention and partnership in supporting [Child's Name]. I look forward to working together to ensure [he/she/they] can thrive in school.

> Sincerely,
>
> [Your Name]
>
> [Your Contact Information]

2. **Parent Input Statement / Letter for IEP or 504 Meeting**

Subject: Parent Input Statement for [Child's Name] – [Date of Meeting or School Year]

Dear [Case Manager's Name / IEP Team / 504 Coordinator],

I appreciate the opportunity to share my perspective as [Child's Name]'s parent in preparation for our upcoming meeting. My goal is to partner with the school team to ensure [he/she/they] receive the support needed to thrive both academically and emotionally.

A. Strengths and Interests

[Child's Name] is [describe your child's personality—e.g., curious, creative, funny, kind]. [He/She/They] excel in [specific subjects or activities—e.g., math, building projects, storytelling, technology]. [He/She/They] enjoys [list hobbies or motivators—sports, art, video games, reading, music, etc.]. When [he/she/they] feel understood and encouraged, [he/she/they] truly shine.

B. Areas of Challenge

Some areas where [Child's Name] continues to need support include:

a) [Attention/focus, reading comprehension, written expression, social skills, organization, etc.]

b) [Provide an example or two of how this shows up in class or at home.]

c) At times, these challenges cause frustration or shutdown, which others may misinterpret as a lack of motivation or defiance. These behaviors often signal that [he/she/they] need help with [specific need—executive functioning, sensory regulation, understanding instructions, etc.].

C. Strategies That Work Well

We've found success with strategies such as:

a) [Examples: visual schedules, chunking tasks, frequent breaks, one-on-one check-ins, quiet work spaces, positive reinforcement, clear instructions, or extra processing time.] These approaches help [Child's Name] stay engaged and confident.

D. **Goals and Hopes for This Year**

My primary goal is for [Child's Name] to feel supported, valued, and understood in the classroom. I hope the team will:

a) Ensure accommodations are implemented consistently across subjects.

b) Foster positive communication between home and school.

c) Support social-emotional learning and self-advocacy skills.

E. **Communication Preferences**

I welcome open communication and appreciate

updates on both progress and challenges. Email is the best way to reach me at [your email address], but I'm also available for brief check-ins as needed.

Thank you for taking the time to review my input and for the ongoing partnership in supporting [Child's Name]. I believe that when we work together, we can help [him/her/them] succeed not only academically but also in confidence and self-belief.

Warm regards,

[Your Full Name]

[Your Contact Information]

Parent of [Child's Name]

3. Sample Email: Addressing a Violation or Unmet Accommodations

Subject: Concern Regarding Implementation of [Child's Name]'s 504/IEP Accommodations

Dear [Teacher or Case Manager's Name],

I'd like to bring to your attention some concerns about the implementation of [Child's Name]'s [504 Plan/IEP]. I've noticed that [describe what's missing — e.g., extended test time not being provided, breaks not allowed, assignments not modified].

I would appreciate the opportunity to discuss how we can ensure the accommodations outlined in [his/her/their] plan are consistently implemented. Please let me know a good time to meet or call this week.

Thank you for your partnership and continued support of [Child's Name].

Warm regards,

[Your Name]

4. Formal Letter to a Superintendent or Grievance Office

Subject: Formal Grievance – Failure to Implement 504/IEP or Discriminatory Practices

Dear [Superintendent's Name],

I am writing to file a formal grievance regarding the failure to provide appropriate accommodations and supports for my child, [Child's Name], under [Section 504/IDEA]. Despite multiple attempts to resolve this issue at the school level, the situation remains unresolved.

Specifically, [briefly describe what happened — e.g., your child was repeatedly denied accommodations, disciplined unfairly, or removed from class in violation of their plan]. These actions have significantly impacted [his/her/their] ability to access an equitable education.

I request a formal review and written response within the district's established grievance timeline.

Please confirm receipt of this letter and outline the next steps in the review process.

Sincerely,

[Your Name]

[Your Address]

[Your Phone/Email]

Questions to Ask in Meetings

During an Evaluation Meeting

- What data did the team use to determine eligibility?

- How are the results being interpreted in relation to classroom performance?

- What interventions have we already tried, and what were the results

- How will progress be monitored and communicated to me?

During a 504 or IEP Meeting

- Which accommodations or goals will best support my child's current challenges?

- How will teachers ensure they use these accommodations daily?

- How often will the plan be reviewed or adjusted?

- What supports are available for emotional regulation or executive functioning?

When Things Aren't Working

- Who is responsible for implementing this part of the plan?

- How can I request an addendum meeting before the following annual review?

- What documentation should I provide to support my concerns?

- What are the next steps if I disagree with the team's decision?

www.ingramcontent.com/pod-product-compliance
Lightning Source LLC
Chambersburg PA
CBHW071430130726
47997CB00006B/2020